0006591

COLLIN COUNTY COMMUNITY

S0-BSK-222

Learning Resources Center
Collin County Community College District

WITHDRAWN

Plano, Texas 75074

WILMMOB99

NB
1272   Williams, Guy R.
W5
        Making mobiles

$9.95

© THE BAKER & TAYLOR CO.

Making Mobiles

BOOKS BY GUY R. WILLIAMS

Paint Now, Learn Later
Working with Leather
Making Mobiles

GUY R. WILLIAMS

Making Mobiles

EMERSON BOOKS, INC.
Buchanan, New York 10511

Remember that the most beautiful things in the world
are the most useless; peacocks and lilies for instance.
John Ruskin, *The Stones of Venice*, Vol. I

Published 1969 by Emerson Books, Inc.
Library of Congress Catalog Card Number 76–76580
Standard Book Number 87523–167–5
Copyright © Guy R. Williams 1968
All rights reserved
Printed in the United States of America

Fourth Printing, 1979

Contents

List of plates

1

What is a mobile?

What, first, does the word 'mobile' mean? A standard dictionary offers this definition: Capable of movement; moveable; not fixed or stationary.

Since that dictionary was compiled, the word has gained an extra meaning. Now, it is applied freely to all works of art that depend in the slightest upon movement of any kind for their appeal. Mobiles—hanging from the ceilings of shops, swaying in the foyers of hotels, scintillating with light and cheer at Christmas—are definitely part of the contemporary scene. And it is entirely appropriate that this should be so, for we are living in an era when movement, travel and speed are subjects in the forefront of most people's minds; when anything static has to be extremely good—or extremely bad—if it is to claim any attention at all. Now, with fearless men journeying into space and encircling the earth in a matter of minutes, with inter-planetary cruises being planned and with the moon apparently waiting to be landed upon, men, women and children are more conscious of orbits, space–time relationships and the wonders of astronomy than in any previous period. It is hardly surprising that the moving models in the Science Museum, South Kensington, London are now among the capital's most popular tourist attractions.

Mobiles, then, capture exactly the flavour of our age. But not all the many mobiles we see around are likely to have been produced by professional artists. Many of them will have been created, arranged, devised—whichever word is the most apt—by commercial display technicians, interior decorators, amateur craftsmen and other inventive persons. Only a very small percentage of them are likely to have more than a brief and ephemeral existence. It is the very ease with which mobiles can be produced that makes them ideal subjects for study in the school and in the home, as well as in the studio.

This book is intended to show that mobile-making can be one of the most enjoyable hobbies that can be pursued. It is a hobby that calls for no items of equipment that are difficult to find, need not consume any expensive materials, and demands little manual skill. One or two of the simplest examples described in the early pages of this book can be cut out, assembled, and made to work in the course of a single evening. If, after making a few of these elementary mobiles, you decide to embark on some more ambitious projects—several kinds are examined in the later pages—you will find that the interest they arouse is out of all proportion to the care you have had to expend on them. As Robert Louis Stevenson said: 'For my part, I travel not to go anywhere, but to go. I travel for travel's sake. The great affair is to move.'

2

Credit where credit is due

There is no reason why you should read this chapter if you have picked up this book only in order to learn how to make mobiles. If you are not interested in the historical background of this interesting hobby, skip on immediately to Chapter 3. Perhaps, then, you may get the urge to turn back to this page when you have made a few mobiles successfully, and would like to know how they were first developed.

It is often said that Alexander Calder invented mobiles. The idea that one man alone has been responsible for a major event in art history is one that can be guaranteed to appeal to people with romantic natures. Certainly, no one else could have a better claim than Calder to that distinction, but the use of the word 'invented' is an over-simplification that may be misleading, so here is a brief description of the artistic scene as it was before Calder made his ingenious experiments. The proper importance of those experiments cannot be easily understood unless one has some slight knowledge of the conditions under which they were carried out.

First, it has to be borne in mind that other people, before Calder, had found movement fascinating, and had tried to exploit their interest in various ways, many of which you will find worthy of study if you intend to take up mobile-making seriously. Among the ingenious devices that may be fairly thought to have foreshadowed

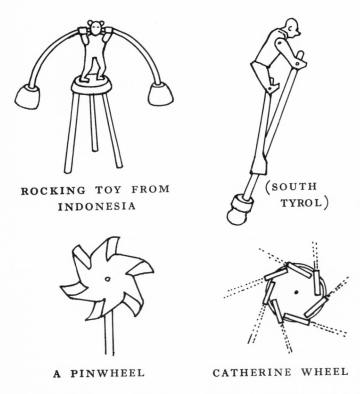

ROCKING TOY FROM
INDONESIA

(SOUTH
TYROL)

A PINWHEEL   CATHERINE WHEEL

Fig 1. *Some moving toys that preceded the mobile*

mobiles were certain historical childrens' toys. Particularly stimulating were the small articulated figures that tumbled up and down ladders, counterbalanced toys that rocked or swung backwards and forwards with the gentle regularity of a pendulum, gravity-operated mechanical dolls, spinning tops of various kinds, marionettes and other line-operated puppets, stick puppets, autogyroes that could be made to remain poised magnificently on a point for a long period of time by a sharp tug on a string, and the miniature race-horses that could be made to move forward towards a winning post by being placed on a vibrating cloth; kites and wind-operated pinwheels or 'windmill sticks' that still intrigue children, as they have done for many centuries, and certain fireworks, especially the fast-rotating 'Catherine wheels'.

Then it must be remembered, too, that Calder, as a young man, could hardly have failed to be aware of the great scientific discoveries that had been made in the last decades of the nineteenth century and the first decades of the twentieth.

The extensive researches made by the great physicists of the world had revealed that 'solid' matter is not really as solid as it appears, and that even substances as hard and as apparently impenetrable as iron, rock and glass are made up of billions of tiny molecules, each of which, in its turn, consists of a number of rapidly-moving atoms. These revelations made many people more con-scious of movement than their ancestors had been, and this new interest was given extra stimulus by several astronomical events of outstanding importance. The most notable of these was, perhaps, the re-appearance of Halley's Comet in 1910, the total solar eclipses seen in 1925 in parts of North America, and in parts of Northern Europe in 1927, and the discovery, at Flagstaff Observatory in 1930, of the planet now named Pluto, near the position predicted by the late Percival Lowell. After those occurrences, it would have been difficult for any sensitive artist to confine his attention entirely to

Fig 2. *A well-known lady (left) seen in a Cubist's
sketchbook (right)*

still life paintings and static landscapes. All artists,
however parochial their subject matter, tended to become
subtly involved in the workings of the universe.

The first major works of art that bear obvious traces
of the new unrest were certain Cubist paintings produced
in France shortly before the First World War. Before
executing these, artists such as Georges Braque, Pablo
Picasso and Juan Gris had decided that it was no longer
necessary, or even desirable, to represent solid forms in
a painstakingly naturalistic way. Instead, they tried to
describe those forms by a new and up-to-date method—
they attempted to break each of the forms down by
careful analysis into a complex series of inter-related
planes. The geometric and repetitive nature of the
works that resulted was thought by many observers to
be entirely appropriate to an age in which motor cars
and other machine-made articles were being brought
increasingly into everyday use. There was little room in
such a functional era, the artists seemed to be saying,

for any mysterious, sensuous or sentimental reminders of the nineteenth century.

After the Cubists came the Futurists (the two groups were working concurrently for some years). The Futurists were dynamic men who loved action, speed, and—less happily, perhaps—violence. For them, energetic movement was a vital element in a picture or piece of sculpture. Unfortunately for them, the materials traditionally used for painting and sculpture are inert, or almost so, and this poses certain technical problems for artists who wish to choose moving people, animals

Fig 3. A Siamese cat sketched by a Futurist

or vehicles as their subjects. How, for example, could a painter who claimed to be a Futurist represent convincingly with oil colours, water colours or pastels a racing car travelling at one hundred miles an hour? How could a sculptor carve from a block of wood or marble a galloping horse that really looked as if it were galloping, and not merely as if it had been caught in a single attitude and solidified? Most of the Futurist-painters used to solve this problem (or partly solve it) by borrowing a technical device from the cinema—they would show the car (or horse, or whatever moving person, creature or object they were trying to represent) not once on the flat surface of a sheet of paper or canvas, but many times, allowing the images to overlap so that the impression given to the viewer was as blurred and as inexact as the sight of a real speeding vehicle would be.

Futurist sculptors had no easy solution (or part-solution) at hand. Usually, they attempted to suggest

Fig 4. The Shark; swift movement under water expressed by a sculptor influenced by the Futurists

violent movement or activity by allowing the forms they modelled, carved or fabricated to multiply, merging them, often, into each other so that their works began to look like three-dimensional versions of the flat, repeated images of the graphic Futurists.

And so, with the more progressive artists of Europe and America favourably inclined towards novel and possibly revolutionary experiments, with the Constructivists led by Naum Gabo advocating that new sculpture should be created in terms of space and organized air, the stage was properly set for the dramatic entrance into international art affairs of Alexander Calder.

Calder was born in Philadelphia, Pa., in the year 1898. Like many artists of note he was brought up in a cultured atmosphere, his father and grandfather both being sound academic sculptors, his mother being a painter of some distinction. As a young man, he showed a strong inclination towards mechanical engineering, and, in fact, he graduated successfully in that field at the Stevens Institute of Technology, Hoboken, New Jersey. Instead of attempting to make a living as a mechanical engineer, though, Calder went on to study painting under John Sloan and Boardman Robinson at the Art Students League in New York.

When his drawing had become sufficiently proficient, Calder started to work regularly for the New York *Police Gazette*, supplying studies of boxers, acrobats, and other picturesque subjects for publication in that journal's pages. His searches for suitable material took him frequently to the circus, where the brilliant colours, the glamorous lighting and the dazzling virtuosity of the performers exerted an understandable fascination over him. Using the skills he had acquired during his training as an engineer, Calder set out to construct a model circus with miniature replicas of the performers, from pieces of wood, cork, wire and other oddments. It can be convincingly argued that here, in this little mechanical plaything that delighted all his friends was the germ from which all Calder's later work was to develop.

In 1926, Calder left the United States and went to Paris—a step taken by many promising young American artists at that time. Shortly after he arrived there, he went to see Piet Mondrian, an artist who had banished all forms of representation from his work. Calder found Mondrian's abstract, geometric designs—carried out, principally, in black and white and brilliant primary colours—extremely exciting, and soon the young American was carrying out wire 'sculptures' that incorporated flat geometric shapes not unlike those used by Mondrian. It was a logical step, then, for Calder to make these shapes move by simple mechanical means in much the same way as he had animated his miniature circus artists. Each sculpture, of course, moved in a planned and pre-determined way.

The next step Calder took was not so logical—in fact, it was the result of a happy inspiration, when he literally 'harnessed the winds' and allowed chance movements of air currents to provide the activating forces for some especially light sculptures that were allowed to hang freely. This was, in practice, the birth of the mobile as we know it today. Calder's earliest mobiles, exhibited in the Galerie Vignon and other galleries, excited immediate interest, and soon people in many parts of the world were experimenting with the technique which the young American had developed. The French artist Duchamp is usually given the credit for first applying the word 'mobile' to Calder's early work.

3

Making a start
What you will need

There is little point in describing in length at this stage the tools needed for advanced work, since every mobile designer who is working in a personal and original way will want to evolve his or her own techniques. Some sculptors are not really happy unless they are working with fibreglass, others only become truly creative when they are standing by a forge. If you are a beginner, you will probably be content with the enchanting mobiles you can make from some short pieces of thread and the interesting shapes you can cut with a knife or a pair of scissors from a sheet of thin card or mounting board. Later, you will be able to experiment with wire and other metal components.

SOMEWHERE TO WORK

There is no reason why mobiles of a considerable size should not be made and assembled in an ordinary living room or craft room. In domestic surroundings you will find it easier to work methodically if you have a firm flat surface on which to rest your components while you are preparing them for assembly. A work bench is ideal, but a strong table should make a perfectly adequate substitute. If your working surface is of a kind that can

Learning Resources Center
Collin County Community College District
SPRING CREEK CAMPUS
WITHDRAWN

be easily spoiled by being scratched, scored or stained, cover it with several sheets of newspaper or a thick cloth before you put anything on it.

THE TOOLS YOU WILL NEED

Here is a brief list of tools you may find useful when you are making simple mobiles. You may not need all of them

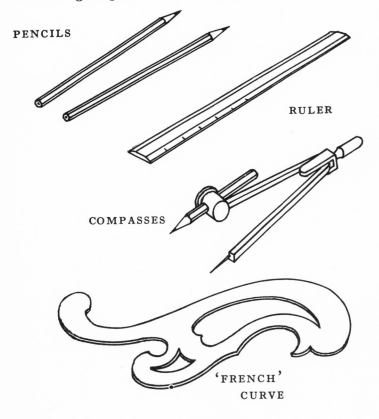

PENCILS

RULER

COMPASSES

'FRENCH' CURVE

Fig 5. Drawing instruments

—there are few hobbies that demand a smaller outlay.
Drawing instruments. A sharp pencil is almost essential
for marking out the flat components of a simple mobile.
Pencils are marketed in a number of grades of hardness
and softness, the medium grades H and HB being as
useful as any. A ruler is quite indispensable for drawing
straight lines and for taking measurements.

Many mobiles contain shapes that are wholly or
partly circular. For drawing these, you will need a pair
of compasses (though it is possible to use a coin or a
plate, or some other circular object to guide your pencil).
A French curve or draughtsman's curve will come in
useful when subtly curved silhouettes are to be drawn
with a pencil.

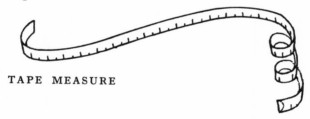

TAPE MEASURE

Fig 6. *For measuring*

Measuring implements. A tape measure—the kind used
by dressmakers—may be used instead of, or as well as,
a ruler. It will certainly be useful when you need, later,
to measure curved lengths of wire.
Cutting implements. A pair of scissors may be used for
cutting out (and trimming) card and mounting board
components. Alternatively, a sharp knife can be used—
an X-acto knife or a mounting knife with replaceable
blades would be suitable. Double-edged razor blades
are liable to cut the fingers; single-edged steel-backed
blades are safer.

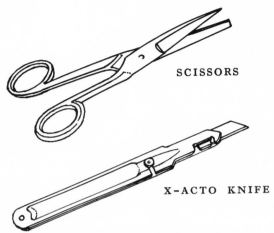

SCISSORS

X-ACTO KNIFE

Fig 7. *Cutting implements*

Painting implements. The question of colour in mobiles will be dealt with later, in Chapter 5. Assuming that you will be wanting to colour some at least of the components in your mobiles you will need at least one paintbrush. A soft, flat brush about one inch across will be generally suitable.

BRUSHES, FOR
COLOUR

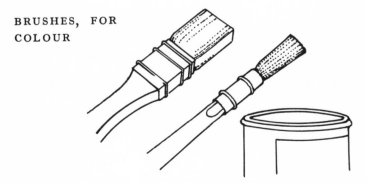

Fig 8. *Suitable paint brushes*

Other implements. Other implements that may be useful are paper clips, 'crocodile' clips (the kind used by radio technicians), and any other small items of equipment normally found in the home or garage.

MATERIALS NEEDED FOR THE SIMPLEST MOBILES

Card. One of the best kinds of card to use for small, simple mobiles is plain white mounting board, since this does not usually warp in a disappointing and unsightly way when it has been cut. Some 'fashion boards' are just as good. Thinner cards (as, for example, postcards) can be used for very small mobiles, but they lack the rigidity needed, surprisingly enough, for larger moving components!

Other materials. It would be unwise to recommend any other materials too exactly, since it is possible to put to good use so many other kinds that may come to hand unexpectedly in the ordinary routines of a household. Spring cleaning, for example, may produce a pile of unwanted cards and folders that would be ideally suited for conversion by a little imaginative trimming into bird, fish or purely abstract shapes, and these could look most attractive when combined according to the methods shortly to be described into a moving composition. The clearing of a cluttered loft or garage may bring back a number of forgotten mechanical parts—from an old clock or musical box, perhaps— that are so light and elegant that they might have been specially designed for use in a decorative mobile. Pieces of plastic sheet, metal oddments and bits of glass, as well as wood, veneers, balsa wood, shells, feathers and other natural forms may also be collected to provide the basic materials for some most interesting mobiles.

4

Mobiles from paper and card

It is not a good idea to start mobile-making by choosing materials that are at all difficult to manipulate. It is wiser for the beginner to get used, first, to constructing effective and exciting examples from paper, card and other light, easily cut, easily shaped and easily joined materials. More demanding techniques, such as those in which wire and sheet metal are used, can come later.

MAKING A PINWHEEL

You could start by making a simple pinwheel, like the one shown in illustration 1. If it is fastened to a stick so that it is free to rotate, a pinwheel of this kind will make an amusing gift for a child.

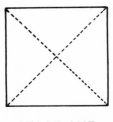
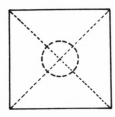

STAGE ONE   STAGE TWO

Fig 9. *Making a pinwheel (first stages)*

Begin by taking a piece of paper (or very thin card) that is 3 ins. or 4 ins. square. Then mark it off as shown in illustration 9. The diameter of the circle at the centre can be a little larger than that of a half dollar. Then cut a circular piece of cardboard and paste or glue it over this circle (this is for strengthening the centre of the pinwheel).

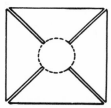

Fig 10. *Making a pinwheel—four slits*

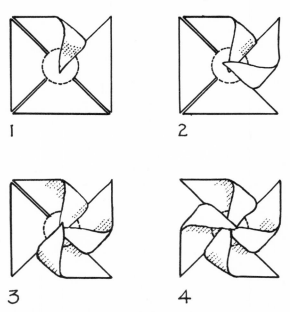

Fig 11. *Making a pinwheel (later stages)*

Then cut four slits along the diagonals, as shown in illustration 10. This produces a shape known frequently as a 'Maltese' cross. Each arm of the cross has two outer corners. Take one corner of each arm (in every case, the same corner), ease it gently over the centre of the wheel, and paste or glue it down, as shown in illustration 11.
When the adhesive is dry, make a hole at the centre that passes through all four of the stuck-down corners, pass a pin, nail or piece of wire through this hole (which must be large enough to allow the wheel to rotate freely), fix it to a suitable stick or post, and allow the wind to play on the back of the wheel.

A pinwheel that is a little more complicated (and also a little more decorative) can be made from a hexagon or six-sided figure. To construct the hexagon, draw a

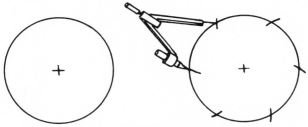

Fig 12. *Constructing a hexagon*

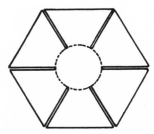

Fig 13. *A pinwheel based on a hexagon—the slits*

circle, and then, without altering the set of the compasses, mark off the radius six times around the circumference, as shown in illustration 12. Then make a small inner circle as before, reinforce it with card, and make six slits inwards from the corners, as shown in illustration 13.

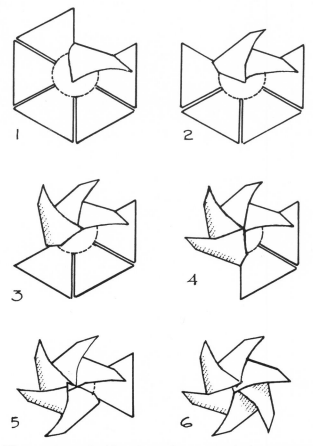

Fig 14. *A pinwheel based on a hexagon—the later stages*

To complete the pinwheel, bring alternate corners over to the centre and secure them again, as before (illustration 14). A small slit has to be made in the last arm so that this corner will fit neatly into position. This pinwheel, too, should be fixed to a suitable stick or post.

A SPIRAL MOBILE

Above any warm stove or radiator there will normally be an upward current of air. This air, as it rises, can be used to keep a small spiral mobile turning. Playthings of this sort have been made for hundreds of years to amuse children, but it is only recently that the name 'mobile' has been applied to them.

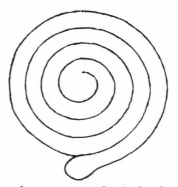

Fig 15. *A paper or card spiral—the outline*

To make a spiral mobile of this kind, take a piece of stout cartridge paper or thin card and draw on it the shape that you are going to cut out (illustration 15). The width of the spiral strip should be uniform. If you find it difficult to draw, illustration 16 may help. Then

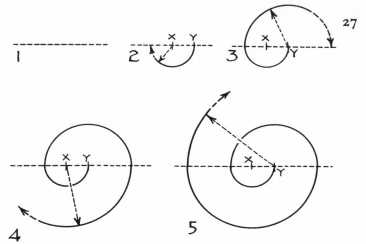

Fig 16. *This shows how a spiral can be drawn with a pair of compasses. Starting with a straight line (1) and then a half-circle (2) the spiral is developed with further half circles. The centre points of these are (3) Y, (4) X, (5) Y and so on, X and Y being used alternately*

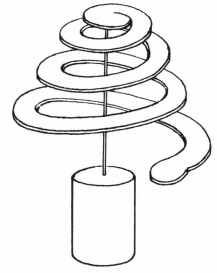

Fig 17. *The paper or card spiral in action—as a mobile*

cut out the shape, leaving the central portion uncut so that it will provide a flat disc round the point of balance. Arrange some convenient pivot on which the spiral can revolve—a large cork with a needle or a knitting needle stuck into it may be suitable. Balance the spiral on the point, place it in a rising current of air, and it should go on turning merrily for as long as there is any warmth to provide the motive power. Alternatively, of course, a spiral of this kind can be suspended by a thread from a fixing immediately above the point of balance.

BEND   BEND
FORWARD   BACK

Fig 18. *A figure is added to the spiral*

Extra interest and amusement can be added to a spiral mobile of this kind if a small and possibly grotesque figure is drawn on some stiff card, cut out, and fixed in an upright position on the central platform. Tabs, beneath the feet of the figure, will make it easy to glue **an** addition of this kind in place.

CONCENTRIC RINGS

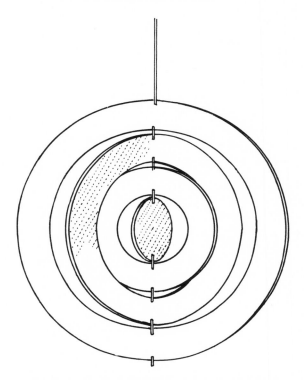

Fig 19. *A mobile based on concentric rings*

It need take you only a matter of moments to make the amusing mobile shown in illustration 19. If it is hung in a place in which there are moving currents of air the concentric rings of which the mobile is composed will move round their common vertical axis quite indepen-dently of each other, making an ever-changing series of delightful shapes for the eye to rest on.

Begin by drawing seven circles on a sheet of thin,

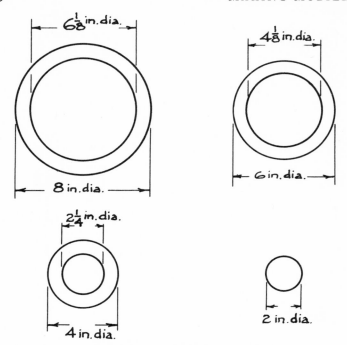

Fig 20. *The component parts of the mobile in fig* 19

strong card. The sizes of these circles are shown in
illustration 20. Six of them are arranged in pairs so that
they will form, when cut out, a series of three rings. The
seventh and smallest circle, when cut out, will be used
as the central component of the mobile.

When you have cut out the rings, lay them on a clean
flat working surface so that the central component is
inside the smallest ring, the smallest ring is inside the
next smallest, and so on. This is shown on the left of
illustration 21.

Then put a ruler along the diameter of the largest
circle and draw a straight line that passes through the

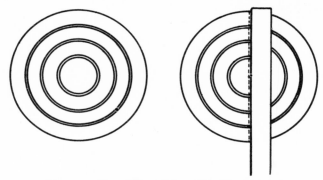

Fig 21. *Assembling the mobile (first stage)*

centre of the central component and extends across all
the other rings to the extreme circumference at either
side. This is shown as a dotted line in the drawing on
the right of illustration 21.

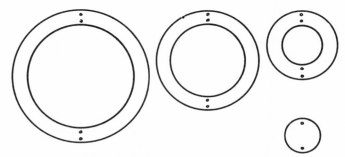

Fig 22. *Preparations for final assembly*

Next, take a pin, a needle, or some other sharp imple-
ment, and make four holes in each ring and two in the
central component. Each of the holes should be on the
line you have just drawn, and each should be a quarter
of an inch from the edge of the card. Illustration 22 shows
these holes.

Then take a needle and a length of thread or cotton,

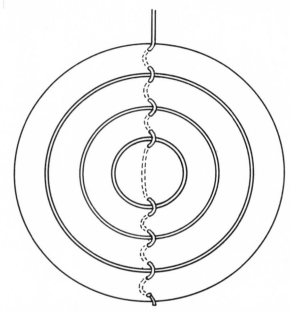

Fig 23. Final assembly, showing position of thread or cotton

pass one end of the thread or cotton through the eye of the needle, and tie a large knot near the other end. Then pass the needle through the holes you have made in the card rings, and in the central component, so that the thread or cotton connects the various parts of the mobile, as shown in illustration 23.

As the last step in the construction of this simple mobile, you will have to fix the thread or cotton so that it remains in the correct position. Small pieces of gummed paper can be used for this, or spots of glue, or both of these together. When the adhesive is dry, the mobile can be suspended in a suitable position so that the rings are free to revolve.

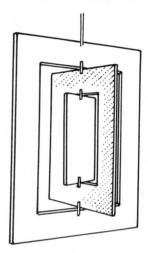

Fig 24. *Another mobile that can be made without difficulty from a piece of card and some thread or cotton*

ANOTHER SIMPLE MOBILE

Another simple mobile that can be made and assembled in much the same way as the last is shown in illustration 24. In this second variation, rectangular forms are used instead of circular rings. Sizes that may serve as a guide to cutting out are suggested in illustration 25. They may be varied in any way that seems desirable. A number of simple mobiles of this kind, hanging over a refreshment table or buffet bar, like those shown in illustration 26, would add considerably to the gaiety of a party. [This brings up the question of colour, which will be dealt with separately in Chapter 5].

It is quite easy—and amusing—to add formal or informal designs to simple mobiles of this kind when they are intended for use as temporary decorations.

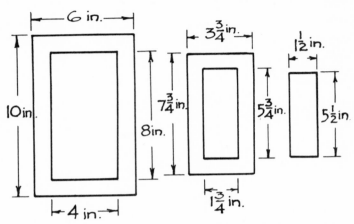

Fig 25. The component parts of the mobile shown in fig 24

Fig 26. Card mobiles used as party decorations

Illustration 27 will give some idea of how the mobile sketched in illustration 24 could be embellished if unbroken white or coloured surfaces were thought too plain.

Fig 27. A card mobile ready to be painted with attractive colours

A MOBILE WITH CARD ARMS

Next, we come to a simple cardboard and thread (or cardboard and string) mobile that may serve as an easy introduction to the projects in the next chapter.

You will need four circles of white or coloured card (made by drawing round a half dollar four times, and cutting round the circumferences of the circles) two small tapering cardboard arms (illustration 28) and one larger arm (illustration 29). Draw out the shape of these

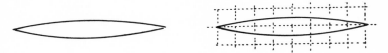

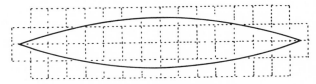

Fig 28. *Two small arms for a card and thread mobile*

Fig 29. *A larger arm*

arms—the dotted squares may help you—cut them out, and make a hole near the end of each arm as shown in illustration 30.

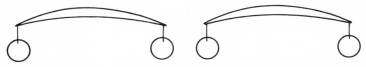

Fig 30. *Position of holes*

Then make a hole near the outer edge of each of the four circular pieces of card, pass a piece of thread through it, and fix the end with a knot, with a spot of glue, or with a small piece of gummed strip. Then allot two of the circles to each of the small arms, and suspend them from the holes at the ends of the arms, as shown in illustration 31.

Fig 31. *The circles suspended from the small arms*

Next, find the point of balance of each of the arms, by trial and experiment (illustration 32).

Fig 32. Finding the point of balance with a compass point or pin

When you are sure that you have found the point of balance, make a hole there, and pass a piece of thread through it—once again, securing the end. To complete the mobile, suspend both of the small arms from the large arm, one at each end, find the point of balance of the large arm, and suspend it in a similar way (illustration 33).

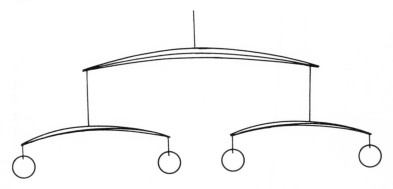

Fig 33. The mobile with card arms, assembled

This will probably encourage you to try making some more ambitious cardboard and thread mobiles, on the

same lines. Illustration 34 shows a most graceful example
made by an East London Grammar School boy, aged
thirteen.

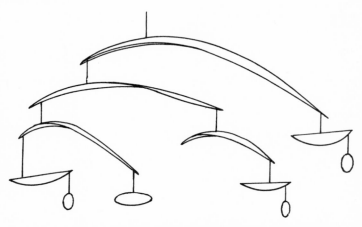

Fig 34. *A well balanced mobile made from cardboard
and thread*

5

Colouring a
simple mobile

Mobiles made of white paper or card may be extremely
attractive, especially when they are seen against a dark
ceiling or background, but colours may be used for a
variety of reasons—to make a more impressive contrast
between the various parts of a mobile and the space or
surfaces behind them; to bring a mobile into a har-
monious relationship with a decorative scheme; to add
extra interest; or to produce any special effect that the
mobile-maker may have in mind. Here are some points
worth remembering:

When colour is used in a mobile, it should be used
definitely, with a clear distinction between the hue,
shade or tint chosen for each part. Subtleties will be
produced by the gentle turns made as the parts move,
and the slight differences in the light and shade of
each part that result.

A mobile that contains black parts as well as white
parts will have the greatest amount of contrast that
can be produced with normal non-luminous pigments,
and it will tend, therefore, to be extra-dramatic and
compelling.

Primary colours—pure blue, red and yellow—and
other bright hues can often be used most successfully

for the moving parts of a mobile. It is not always advisable to try to combine too many of these at any one time, though. A mobile that contains one or more black shapes with a small number of (say) scarlet or crimson shapes will probably be more effective than a mobile that includes shapes in all the colours of the rainbow.

There are several different kinds of paint that are useful to the mobile-maker. Unfortunately, oil-based paints cannot be applied successfully to paper or cardboard unless the surface to be painted has first been treated with size or some other isolating substance so that the oil in the paint will not be absorbed by the fibres of the part being coloured.

Water colours will usually be found to be too thin and transparent, and too lacking in covering power, to be entirely satisfactory.

Poster colours and powder tempera colours can be recommended for paper and cardboard components, with this reservation—they have a tendency to make the thinner and less rigid grades curl or warp out of true, and this can be a distinct disadvantage when flatness is required.

There are two alternative ways of adding colour to a paper or cardboard mobile that are not so likely to result in warping.

The first method involves the purchase of ready-coloured papers and cardboards from a stationer or a supplier of handicraft materials. The usefulness of this method depends, in every case, on the range of suitable materials available. Some suppliers have space to stock only a comparatively limited range.

The second method involves the substitution of

coloured tissue papers for paint. These light papers are now marketed in a wide range of bright and attractive hues and tints, and are quite cheap. They can be pasted down on to a stouter backing, such as that provided by white cardboard, or fixed in position with a rubber-based adhesive. The transparent solutions sold for mounting photographs are specially suitable for fastening pieces of tissue paper to another surface.

Modern manufacturing methods make it possible for scores of different kinds of decorative papers to be produced for packaging purposes, the kinds that imitate gold and silver being particularly suitable for use in decorative mobiles. These can also be collected and fixed to sufficiently strong bases with rubber solution.

Transparent materials, of the cellophane type, can also be obtained in a wide range of colours, some of which are as rich as those to be found in the most impressive stained glass windows. Mobiles made with these materials look particularly attractive when they are placed near a source of light and may spread a cheerful glow or a gay kaleidoscope of moving colours over a large area of wall, floor or ceiling surface. Tough acetate films (known, usually, as 'cinemoid gels') are sold for stage lighting purposes and can be trimmed to any desired shape with a sharp pair of scissors.

Unfortunately, metal shapes cannot always be coloured as easily and as quickly as paper and cardboard surfaces, but some technical notes that may be useful will be found in Chapter 8.

6

Making mobiles
with wire

Wire is one of the most useful materials available to the
mobile-maker. Many types are marketed, the kind that
is most useful for small and medium-sized mobiles being
known as 'galvanized iron wire.' The following thicknesses are recommended:

> 12 S.W.G. — 0·104 in.
> 14 S.W.G. — 0·080 in.
> 16 S.W.G. — 0·064 in.
> 18 S.W.G. — 0·048 in.

(The letters 'S.W.G.' stand for 'Standard Wire
Gauge'). Heavier wire may be acquired when a job calls
for greater strength.

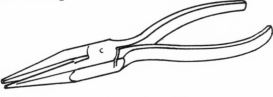

Fig 35. Round-nosed pliers

For bending wire, and manipulating it generally, a
pair of round-nosed pliers is ideal (illustration 35).

Usually, a pair of pliers of this kind will incorporate a cutter that has been specially designed for snipping wire to length. A pair of side-cutting nippers can, of course, be used instead.

A SIMPLE MOBILE MADE WITH WIRE

Here is a step-by-step account of the processes by which a small, decorative, wind-activated mobile can be produced. You will need four lengths of galvanized iron wire—16 S.W.G. is recommended. Cut the wire to these lengths: 11 in., 14 in., 15 in. and 18 in. and file the ends so that they are perfectly smooth.

Then bend each of the pieces of wire so that it retains a very slight curve. This is a procedure often followed by mobile-makers who wish their mobiles to be especially graceful—arms that have been carefully eased into shallow arcs being in general much more suitable for moving compositions than straight arms, which tend to be rather formal and static.

It is fairly easy to form a smooth curve in a piece of 16 S.W.G. or 18 S.W.G. wire, but the whole length should be treated at once. Simply grip one end of the wire with your left hand—if you are right handed—and pull the rest of the wire gently between the thumb and forefinger of your right hand. Repeat this procedure a few times, easing the wire almost imperceptibly into shape as you do so. If you try to bend one part only of the wire at a time, you are most likely to produce an arm marred by kinks and erratic curves. Should you be forced to use wire that has already a number of kinks in it, try to get it quite straight before you form the curve you want. Tapping gently with a hammer is one method, but this does call for a certain amount of experience.

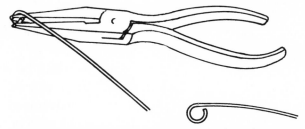

Fig 36. Making a loop at the end of a wire arm

Next, make small loops at the ends of the arms so that you can attach, later, cut-out pieces or shapes to them. Use a pair of round-nosed pliers to make the loops, and turn the wire so that the eyelets you make will be on the underside of the arms when the arms have been assembled. Leave the loops, at first, very slightly open. They can be closed, later, when the mobile has been finally assembled. [Illustration 36].

Fig 37. A circular disc, ready to be assembled in a simple mobile made with wire

For a simple but effective mobile you can make circular shapes to hang at the ends of the arms. Draw eight circles, each $2\frac{1}{2}$ in. diameter, on a piece of card and cut them out. Then pierce each of them once with a pin or needle, to make a small hole about $\frac{1}{4}$ in. from the edge. Push the end of a piece of thread, cotton, or thin wire

1. Alexander Calder. 'Antennae
with Red and Blue Dots'.
*Reproduced by permission of the
Director of the Tate Gallery,
London*

2. Alexander Calder. 'Standing Mobile'. Painted red, yellow, white, black and brass. *Reproduced by kind permission of the Brook Street Gallery, London*

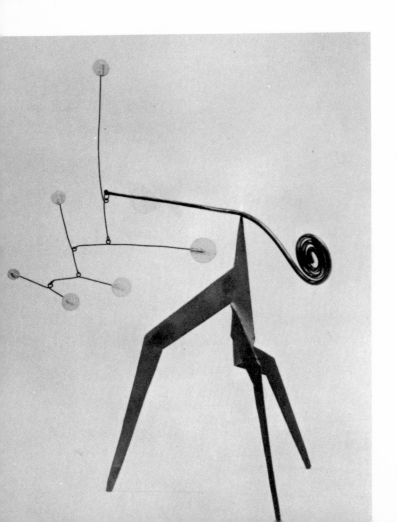

3. Alexander Calder. 'Le Rouge, Le Noir et Le Blanc'. Painted metal mobile, 1964. This mobile was included in the 'Art and Movement' Exhibition organized by the Scottish Committee of the Arts Council of Great Britain in 1965. *Reproduced by kind permission of the Brook Street Gallery, London*

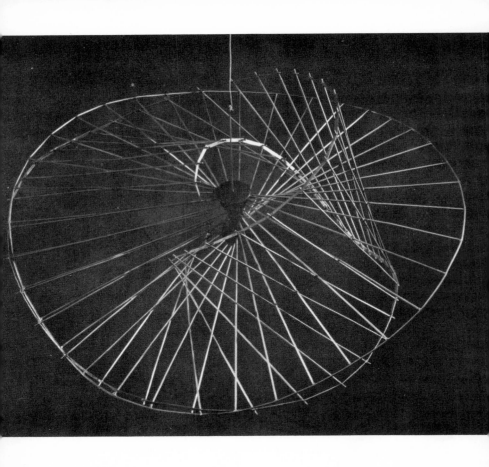

4. Kenneth Martin. 'Screw Mobile with Black Centre'. *Reproduced by permission of the Director of the Tate Gallery, London*

through each of the holes, and tie it or twist it so that it makes a small loop. A circular disc, ready to be incorporated in the mobile, is shown in illustration 37.

Fig 38. The assembly of the first arm

Next you can start to build or assemble the mobile.

Almost invariably, it is best to begin with the lowest arm, and to work upwards, so take the shortest piece of wire and suspend two of the cardboard discs from it, one at each end, as shown in illustration 38.

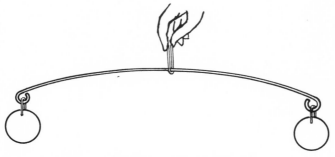

Fig 39. Finding the point of balance

Then find the point on the arm at which it may be suspended in a state of equilibrium. There is an easy way of doing this—simply slip a piece of cotton or thread round the wire and hold it up so that it hangs freely. If the arm tips down on either side, move the cotton or thread along until the arm remains in perfect balance. The point of suspension is, then, the one at

which you will wish to make the first loop for attachment. (As an alternative method, try gripping the arm
lightly in the pliers until the correct point of balance has
been found). Illustration 39 shows the first method.

*Fig 40. How to make a loop at the point of balance, in
four stages (the dotted lines show the position of the
round-nosed pliers used to grip the wire)*

To make the loop, grip the wire at the point of balance
with the tip of your round-nosed pliers and then bend
the two free lengths over the pliers so that a small eyelet
is formed, as shown in illustration 40. Care should be
taken to ensure that this eyelet will eventually be on the
upper side of the arm. If the eyelet has been neatly made,
the whole arm should have regained its former gentle
curve by the time the operation is finished—with, of
course, the addition of the relatively unobtrusive eyelet.

Next, take the piece of wire that is to form the second

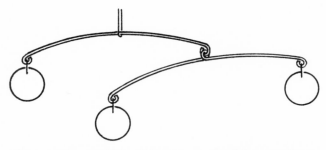

Fig 41. The assembly of the first arm and the second arm

arm of the mobile. Coax it into a smooth curve as you
did the first, and make a small loop at each end for
attachment purposes.

Then assemble the first arm and the second arm, in
this way:

First, hang another cardboard disc from one of the
attachment loops on the second arm.

Then hang the first arm from the second arm, using
for this purpose the unoccupied attachment loop on the
second arm. Illustration 41 shows how the two arms
should look when they are together.

Then put a piece of thread or cotton round the second
arm, and find the point at which it may be suspended in
a state of equilibrium. You may decide to remove the
first arm temporarily while you make an attachment
loop at the point of balance in the second. Re-assemble
the two arms, when you have made the loop, and they
should hang easily from a thread passed through the
upper attachment loop.

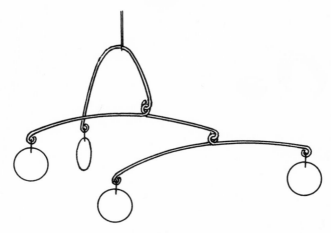

Fig 42. The third arm is added

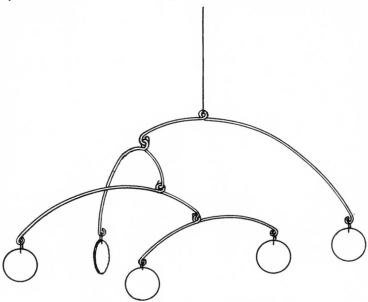

Fig 43. *The complete mobile*

The third arm and the fourth arm are made and assembled in exactly the same way as the second. Make an attachment loop at each end of the third arm, hang a card disc from one of the loops and the assembly of the first and second arms from the other, find the point of balance, and make an attachment loop on the upper side. Repeat this process with the fourth arm. Illustrations 42 and 43 show the later stages in the production of this mobile.

When the mobile is complete it should be suspended in some position in which it will be subjected to a gentle draught or current of air. The discs should then move round each other in constantly changing orbits, making a really attractive decoration.

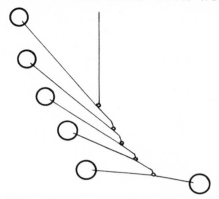

Fig 44. *A beautifully poised wire-and-cardboard mobile*

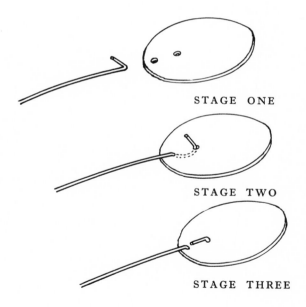

STAGE ONE

STAGE TWO

STAGE THREE

Fig 45. *Attaching components—a standard method*

There are, however, many different kinds of mobile that can be made with wire, and you are not likely to remain satisfied for long with a simple arrangement like the one shown in illustration 43. Next, you may want to try to make and assemble a composition as beautifully poised as the one shown in illustration 44. In this, the circular discs are not allowed to dangle loosely from loops at the ends of the arms. Instead, they are attached by the standard method shown in illustration 45. Two holes are made in each disc, the end of the wire is passed

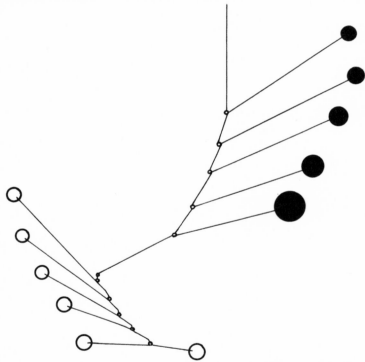

Fig 46. More arms, in this pleasing composition, have been added to the mobile shown in fig 44

through them, and then it is bent back to hold the disc rigidly in place. It helps if the wire is given a preliminary bend before it is passed through the holes.

Illustration 46 shows how a successfully composed mobile of this kind can have further additions made to it, to make it even more ambitious and impressive. These notes may help you, as you experiment:

A mobile may be well balanced, physically, without appearing to be well balanced artistically. You should aim to produce a mobile that is artistically pleasing however it moves, and from whatever viewpoint it is seen. It is not always possible to design a mobile by drawing it on paper first. Often, a mobile that has been carefully planned in two dimensions will prove to be a comparative failure when the design is carried out and seen in three dimensions (i.e., in terms of space).
Some of the most successful mobiles are evolved by piecemeal methods—that is, the appearance and position of the later components is suggested directly by the assembly of the first ones to be made.
In most (though not all) cases, the upper arms of a mobile are made longer than the lower arms, so that the components carried by the higher arms will be kept well clear of the lower components, and fouling will be prevented. Each case, though, must be taken on its individual merits. A glance at the various mobiles illustrated in this book will show how difficult it is to lay down a general rule about such a complex subject.

Finally, in illustration 47, there is shown a mobile, made with wire arms, that incorporates flat components suspended in such a way that they will hang horizontally, instead of vertically.

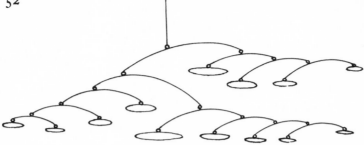

Fig 47. *A mobile with components arranged to hang horizontally*

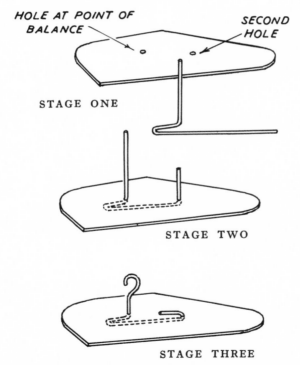

HOLE AT POINT OF BALANCE

SECOND HOLE

STAGE ONE

STAGE TWO

STAGE THREE

Fig 48. *An attachment loop, made with wire, for components that are intended to hang horizontally*

In cases like this, you may find useful the special method of fixing an attachment loop shown in illustration 48. First, find by experiment the point of balance of the component, and make a hole there. Then make a second hole ½ in. or ¾ in. away. Then bend a piece of wire to the shape shown in the upper drawing, put the ends through the holes in the component as shown in the middle drawing, and finish by bending them over as shown in the lowest drawing. There are many possible variations of this method—the main thing to remember when working with wire is that parts intended to move must be allowed to move quite freely or the airy, constantly changing effect of the mobile will be spoiled.

7

Mobiles made with wire
Some possible variations

Although white cardboard discs are suitable for elementary experiments in mobile-making with wire, they have a strictly limited appeal. Once you have acquired the knack of composing mobiles that are artistically pleasing as well as being satisfactorily poised, you will probably want to try some more ambitious variations. In this chapter, a few possible alternatives are described and illustrated. They are intended to stimulate your own ideas, rather than to be regarded as instructions to be literally followed.

A BIRD MOBILE

Birds, fish and other creatures that move naturally in a graceful way are often studied carefully by sculptors, and representations of them are frequently incorporated in simple mobiles, especially in those intended as decorations for nurseries, schools, and other places where young people are gathered together.

Instead of hanging circular pieces of card at the ends of the arms of a mobile of the kind described in the last chapter, you can cut out simple shapes that suggest

54

Fig 49. A bird mobile, made from cardboard and wire,
with threads for suspension

birds (or other natural forms) like those shown in illustration 49. The same method of assembly will be used as for the simple 'abstract' mobiles just described. The birds can be decorated with gay and pleasing colours and can even be given extra interest with glued-on feathers and other embellishments.

If flat cut-out shapes start to pall, you can design more complicated three-dimensional creatures by cutting out two pieces of card for each, and by fitting the two pieces together by means of carefully arranged slits, as shown in illustration 50. The pieces can be given extra strength if strips of paper are bent over to form right-angled supports and are then glued or pasted into the corners of each assembly, as shown in illustration 51.

SLIT
HERE

PIECE ONE

PIECE TWO

←SLIT HERE

Fig 50. *The two pieces that make up the more exciting bird component shown in fig 51*

STRENGTHENING
STRIP

Fig 51. *The assembled cardboard bird*

A FISH MOBILE

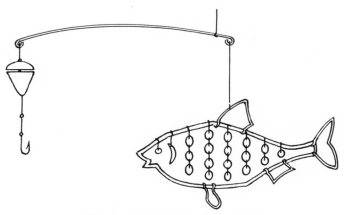

Fig 52. An amusing fish mobile

Illustration 52 shows an amusing fish mobile in which wire is used for making the outline of the main component, as well as for the arm that keeps the fish and the counter-balancing float in equilibrium.

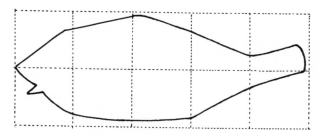

Fig 53. The outline of the main component of the fish mobile shown in fig 52

To make a mobile of this sort, draw the outline of the main component on a piece of paper—the dotted squares in illustration 53 will help you to do this, should you

find it difficult to reproduce the fish on a larger scale.
Make your squares three or four times as large as the
squares in this book, or even larger.

Then bend some stout wire—12 S.W.G. or 14 S.W.G.
would be suitable—until it follows the outline exactly.

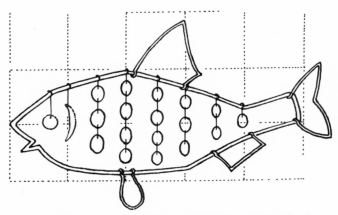

*Fig 54. The main component of the fish mobile—the fins,
tail, eye and 'scales' are added*

Then add the fins and tail by bending lengths of
thinner wire to the required shapes (illustration 54),
securing them by twisting their ends two or three times
tightly round the stouter framework.

Much fun can be had if a search is made for unusual
materials or objects that will serve as the fish's eye, gills
and scales. In the fish shown in the illustration, small
bright metal discs thrown out from a local factory were
fastened together with fine fuse wire and hung from the
upper edge of the fish's frame. As they twisted in the
breeze, they reflected the light brilliantly. Pieces of
glass, clear plastic and other materials can be incorporated to give extra interest or charm to the fish.

A MOBILE WITH DIMINISHING COMPONENTS

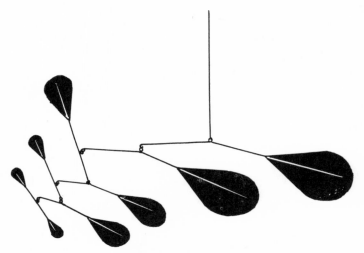

Fig 55. A mobile with diminishing components

An unusually pleasing mobile can be made if some distinctive shape is chosen for the components, each component being made smaller—or larger—than the components next to it (illustration 55). By varying the size of the components according to their position in the mobile, a remarkable effect of spaciousness can be produced—there is an element of 'false perspective' about this that tends to deceive the eye.

A MOBILE MADE WITH PLYWOOD

Illustration 56 shows a mobile made from thin plywood, which is a useful material for the mobile-maker to have available. Even the thinner grades of plywood are heavier than cardboard, so the arms provided for a

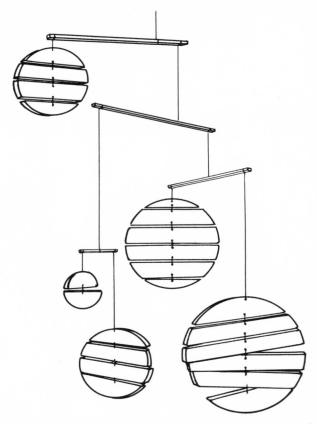

Fig 56. *A mobile made principally from thin plywood*

mobile of this kind have to be made from wire of a
comparatively strong gauge or (as in the illustration)
from lengths of stripwood. As the hanging components,
in this case, are initially circular, the straight rigidity of
the stripwood arms makes an effective contrast.

A MOBILE MADE WITH BALSA WOOD

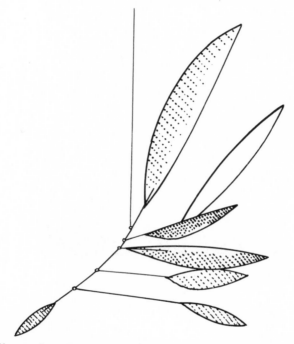

Fig 57. A striking mobile made from wire and balsa wood

Balsa wood, too, is a useful material for the mobile-maker, as it is comparatively light and can be cut and shaped and joined with balsa cement with such ease. Illustration 57 shows how, in a fairly large mobile, balsa wood components can be combined with wire arms to make a component not wholly unlike some exotic succulent plant. Many of the most successful mobiles are reminiscent of living or growing creatures, even if the exact nature of the species that has inspired them cannot be established.

MOBILES FOR CHRISTMAS

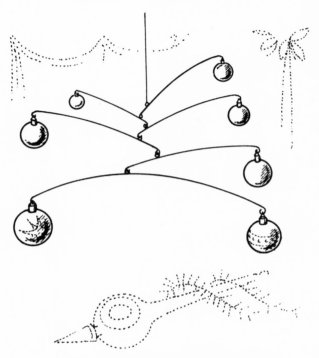

Fig 58. A mobile for Christmas

The weeks immediately before Christmas may not seem the most suitable for mobile-making—most people are much too busy to have any spare time left for hobbies —but if preparations for the festive season are started early enough it may be found convenient to make at least one mobile as part of a carefully mounted decorative scheme. Particularly valuable for this purpose are the bright, colourful spherical decorations sold so cheaply at most stationers' and chain stores. With an outlay of only a small sum on these it is possible to make a mobile (illustration 58) that will be as attractive as any small Christmas tree.

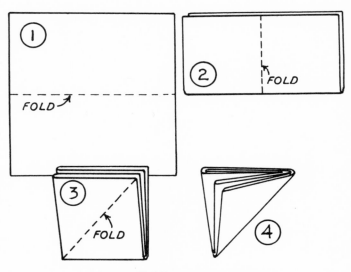

Fig 59. Folding a paper square

Fig 60. The square, folded neatly, is then trimmed

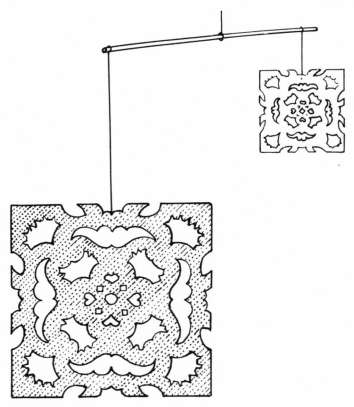

*Fig 61. A decorative mobile, produced by folding and
cutting paper squares*

A CUT-PAPER MOBILE

An attractive form of Christmas decoration uses the
traditional methods of paper folding and paper cutting
still so popular in Poland and certain other parts of
Europe. To experiment with this technique (if you do

not know it already) take a square piece of paper and fold it over three times, as shown in illustration 59. When you have done that, the paper will form a triangle one-eighth the size of the original square.

Then take a sharp pair of scissors and make a few cuts in the triangle, removing certain areas and leaving others uncut. (A knife can be used instead of scissors, if this is preferred, but great care has to be taken if injury is to be avoided). Illustration 60 shows the kind of irregular shape that might be left. Then unfold the paper, and you should find that you have produced a richly ornamental design—possibly, one like the example shown in illustration 61. Cut-out motifs of this kind make splendidly decorative mobiles. If the paper used is not rigid enough, the cut-outs can be stuck to squares of clear plastic or acetate (the kind used by model-makers).

To add variety to cut-out paper mobiles, try folding and cutting circular pieces of paper, instead of square pieces. If you don't enjoy the labour involved, you can buy ready-stamped paper cake-mats or d'oyleys that will add much richness of pattern and texture to a mobile at very little cost.

ANOTHER CHRISTMAS MOBILE

Cut paper decorations of another traditional kind can be incorporated in mobiles at Christmas—if you have the time and the patience to make them.

For each decoration, you will need two circles of coloured paper. Each circle should be marked out and cut like the one shown on the left of illustration 62. If, then, the central portion of each is raised, a lattice-like cone will be formed. By sticking together the outer

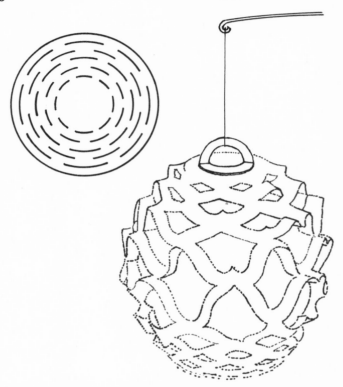

*Fig 62. Another way of making decorative components
for Christmas mobiles—or for mobiles for parties at any
other time of the year!*

edges with spots of adhesive spaced at intervals round
the circumference, the two cones can be combined to
make an egg-shaped decoration well suited for a Christmas mobile. Note, in the illustration, the small card
fitting glued to the top to make hanging possible.

A MOBILE WITH 'SOLID' STARS

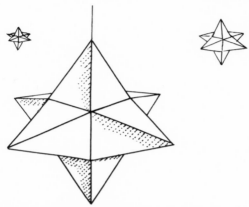

Fig. 63. A 'star' form that would look good in a Christmas
mobile

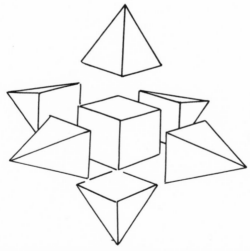

Fig 64. The seven parts that make up the star shown in
fig 63

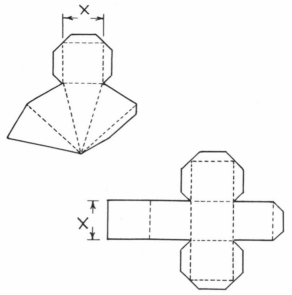

Fig 65. The flattened shapes of the parts shown in fig 64

A mobile which has gold or silver stars suspended and moving in orbit always makes a popular decoration at Christmas time, and illustration 63 shows an apparently solid star (with two others in the background) that can be quite easily made. The seven separate parts from which it is assembled are shown in illustration 64—they are: one cube, made from cut and folded paper, and six identical pyramids, made by the same simple technique. Metallic papers—that is, papers that are specially coated with a gold or silver finish—are ideal for making these stars, though the thinner grades may need to be stiffened with liners cut from card.

Illustration 65 shows how the shapes would look when they are drawn out 'on the flat'. The height of the pyramids—and, therefore, the length of the star's points —is a matter for the designer's taste, but the base of the pyramid—a square—must correspond exactly to the square that is the side of the central cube.

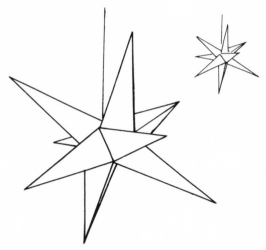

Fig 66. A graceful star based on an octahedron or eight-sided solid

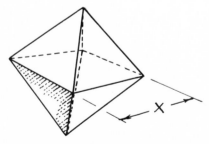

Fig 67. An octahedron (the dimension 'x' must corres-pond with the dimension marked in the same way in the drawing of the star's point, shown in fig 69)

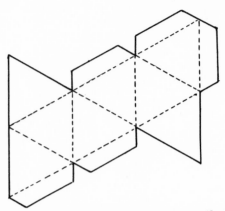

Fig 68. An octahedron can be made quite easily from this 'developed' shape

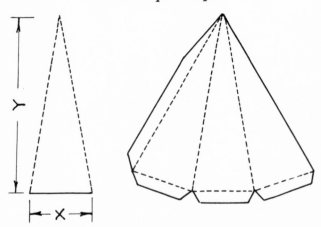

Fig 69. The developed shape of one of the star's points—stage one (above) and stage two (below). The length 'Y' can be any you think suitable

Illustration 66 shows a more graceful star that can be based on an octahedron or eight-sided solid (illustration 67). To make this solid, draw eight equilateral triangles on the flat, as shown in illustration 68, and add five tabs for pasting or gluing after you have cut out the figure and folded along the dotted lines.

Each of the points of the star is drawn on the flat in the way shown in illustration 69, and then cut out, folded along the dotted lines, and pasted or glued to make a solid, as before. A mobile containing these stars could well resemble a constellation made up of stars of several different sizes.

8

Making mobiles
with metal

Making mobiles with metal—in addition to wire—is an
ambitious undertaking for anyone who has had no
training in the elements of metalwork. However, this
chapter is included in case you wish to experiment with
more durable mobiles than those already described.
Mobiles intended to be seen out of doors—garden
mobiles, they might almost be called—will not last very
long if they are made largely from paper or cardboard.

A PLACE TO WORK

People who do a lot of metalwork usually find it convenient to work on a special bench. This will probably
be shorter and narrower than the normal woodwork
bench, and the top surface and the front edge will almost
certainly be made with, or covered with, metal instead
of wood.

If you only intend to work with metal occasionally,
you may be able to adapt one end of a woodwork bench
(or one end of a sturdy old table) to suit these additional
techniques. To do this, cover part of the upper surface
with mild steel sheet—this is especially important if you
intend to solder. A standard metalworker's vice would

be a great asset. If you have already a woodwork vice, which is not by its very nature suitable for holding metal for metalwork, you can screw a metalwork vice to the upper surface of a flat piece of wood. To the underside of the wood, glue and screw a piece of 1 in. × 1 in. strip wood. This strip can then be held firmly in the woodwork vice so that the metalwork vice is given a firm foundation.

If you are going to work with metal on an ordinary household table, remember to cover it with oilcloth first, or with hardboard, or with several thicknesses of newspaper, or you will almost certainly spoil its upper surface.

TOOLS AND EQUIPMENT

Most of the tools you will need when working with metal are to be found in any garage or household maintenance kit, but these are especially important:

Tinmen's Snips or Shears. These are used for cutting sheet metal to shape. You may be offered a straight or

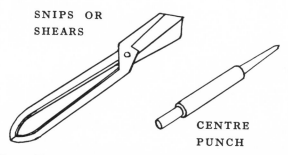

SNIPS OR SHEARS

CENTRE PUNCH

Fig 70. Two tools you will find useful if you make mobiles from metal

curved pair. A pair of universal shears that can be used for cutting straight or curved lines will be most generally useful (illustration 70).

A Hack-saw. Necessary if you intend to cut components from the heavier gauges of sheet metal. Choose a hack-saw with an adjustable frame, if you can. This can be used to hold blades of various sizes.

A Centre Punch. Used for making holes. Invest in a punch that is warranted made of a good quality cast steel, which has been hardened and tempered.

A File.

Less necessary, but still useful are:

A Metal Scriber. Choose one, if possible, with a replace-able point. This can be used, in conjunction with a wooden rule or a special steel rule, for marking out your work.

Spring Dividers. A 3 in. or 6 in. pair may be handy.

METALS IN COMMON USE

The metals generally used by mobile-makers are:

Mild steel. A very malleable (that is, easily hammered) alloy steel, which is easily worked, but is not particularly attractive. Tin plate is more pleasing.

Zinc. Comparatively easy to work, but it is on the heavy side for indoor mobiles and tends to become tarnished rather quickly if exposed to the weather.

Copper. One of the most malleable of metals, it is easy to work and can be hammered to shape even when cold. It tends to be expensive, but it has a lovely warm colour that makes it particularly suitable for use in mobiles where its weight can be properly taken into account. Clear laquers can be bought that will inhibit (or at least slow down) tarnishing.

Brass. An alloy made by combining copper and zinc. It can be drilled, filed, and soldered fairly easily, in spite of being a little harder than unalloyed copper.

Aluminium. A light metal favoured by many mobile-makers. It is quite easy to work, and fairly malleable, but it is not easy to solder unless a special flux is used.

If metals are purchased in *sheet form*, the thickness is shown by the letters S.W.G. (Standard Wire Gauge) in conjunction with a number. This table may help you to translate the more frequently encountered Wire Gauge numbers into decimals of an inch:

S.W.G.	THICKNESS
8	·160
9	·144
10	·128
11	·116
12	·104
13	·092
14	·080
15	·072
16	·064
17	·056
18	·048
19	·040
20	·036

Metal can also be bought (or found on scrapheaps) as *angle iron*, in various lengths in L, U, H or T section, as tubing, and in various prepared forms such as *expanded metal*, *perforated metal*, and various *wire meshes*.

CUTTING METAL

A 10 in. pair of shears will cut metal up to $\frac{1}{16}$ in. thick
with ease. You will soon learn how to handle the shears
so that you can cut a scribed line with a reasonable
amount of accuracy—usually, by making a 'rough cut'
first, wide of the line, followed by an exact trimming cut.
Be careful that you do not snip the palm of your hand
between the handles of the shears as that is quite easily
done and can be painful.

Metals that are too thick to be cut with the snips or
shears need to be cut with a hack-saw. You will probably
find that you are offered blades with 14, 18, 22 or 32
teeth per inch, or a comparable range. If so, choose the
blades with 22 teeth per inch, as those will be most
generally useful.

Check that the cutting edges of the teeth face forward
before you start sawing, otherwise you will ruin that
blade very quickly. And don't try sawing too violently.
A long steady forward stroke, using the whole length
of the blade, will be much more effective than a series of
short sharp vicious jabs.

FILING METAL

When you want to file a metal component exactly to a
scribed line, put it in your vice with the edge to be filed
uppermost, so that about $\frac{1}{4}$ in. of metal projects above the
jaws.

Then stand comfortably with your feet a little apart,
and start to work with the full length of the file, making
slow strokes at an angle of 45° to the metal sheet, or
thereabouts, and applying downward pressure to the
file on the forward strokes only. For most metals used

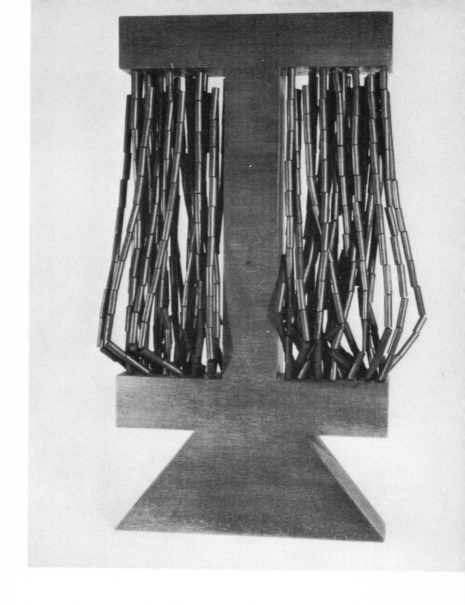

5. Pol Bury. 'Cylindres Enfilés'
1966. A concealed motor keeps the
wooden cylinders moving in this
ominous work of art. *Reproduced
by kind permission of the Kasmin
Gallery, London*

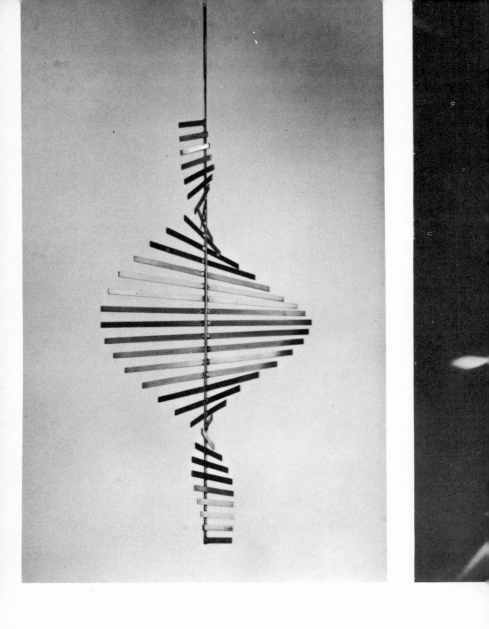

6. Kenneth Martin. 'Small Screw
Mobile 1953'. *Reproduced by
permission of the Director of the
Tate Gallery, London*

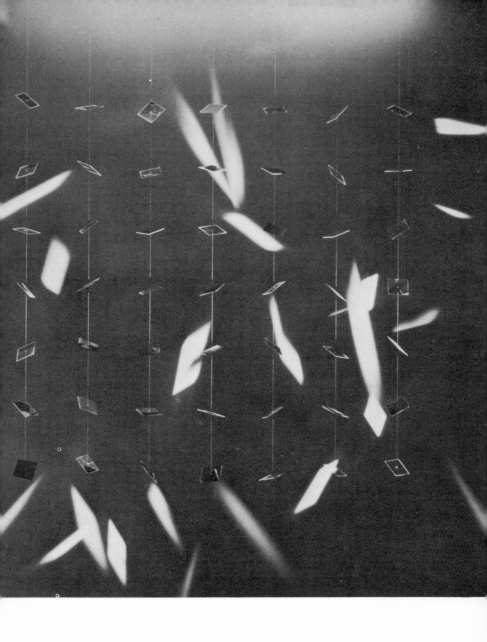

7. J. Le Parc. 'Continuel-Mobile, Continuel-Lumière' 1963. In this, scintillating light is introduced as a contributory factor. *Reproduced by kind permission of the Director of the Tate Gallery, London*

8. Alfred Dunn. 'Quiet Noises' 1967. A small ball
is suspended on a fine thread. Each time it touches
a revolving part, it is sent off on a musical journey,
striking a different note from each of the hanging
bars. *Reproduced by kind permission of the Redfern
Gallery, London*

for mobile-making a 10 in. or 12 in. 'second cut' file is ideal.

You can finish the edge, when it is practically down to the scribed line, with a smoother file. Hold the file with the tips of your fingers and thumbs, and draw it backwards and forwards along the edge of the metal only, instead of across it. This process, which is known as 'draw filing', is shown in illustration 71. It should produce a smooth final surface.

Polish, if you need to, with a piece of emery cloth held round a file and moved in the same way.

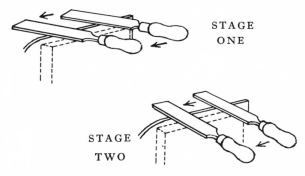

Fig 71. How to file metal components. 'Draw filing' is shown in the lower drawing

BENDING METAL

If you should need to bend or flatten any metal components you will find a hammer and a mallet useful. An engineer's ball pane hammer is ideal, but don't use it for hitting hardened tools such as centre punches or files or you may spoil the striking face, which should be perfectly smooth. While any mallet is better than none for bending and flattening pieces of sheet metal, a beechwood or boxwood mallet is preferred to those made of cheaper woods. Hide-covered mallets are excellent, but they are rather expensive.

To form a right angle bend in a metal component, grip the metal in a vice or between two lengths of angle iron clamped tightly together and use a strip of hardwood to protect the metal from any bruises that could be caused by your hammer. Bend the metal to about 45° to begin with; then work along its whole length, hammering it gently over to the required angle.

SOLDERING

There is no reason why you should find soldering difficult as long as you remember to keep your work absolutely clean, to use the right flux, and to provide the right amount of heat exactly where it is needed.

For most jobs encountered in mobile-making, soft soldering can be used. You can buy ordinary tinmen's solder, which is an alloy of tin and lead, at almost any hardware stores. Don't buy a big block of solder or you will waste a lot of it, besides finding it awkward to handle. The wire-like lengths are more convenient.

Soldering irons are not expensive. The larger sizes keep their heat for a longer time than the smaller ones, but they are more difficult to manipulate. It is best to begin with a fairly small iron.

Flux is needed to make the solder flow properly over the surfaces to be joined. Normally, resin can be used as a flux for soft solders, or tallow, Fluxite or spirits of salts, but there is no reason to remember that, for several good proprietary brands are on sale, and any hardware merchant will advise you. Some solders are sold nowadays with a core of flux inside them, ready for use.

Before you start, make sure that both the pieces of metal to be joined are perfectly clean. File and scrape all surfaces to remove the 'fire skin' present on nearly all hard metals, and use emery cloth to remove all traces of grease. Don't finger the surfaces once you have cleaned them, or you will have to start all over again.

Next, heat up your soldering iron in a gas flame or in the centre of a hot fire. If you have the use of an electric iron, you will only have to plug it in.

As soon as you think the iron is hot enough, put the tip of the iron into the flux. If the bit remains damp when you remove it, the iron is not hot enough. If the flux crackles and pops and gives off a lot of steam the bit is a little too hot. If you think that it is just right, put the solder against it. When the solder has melted, work a thin film of metal over the iron by touching it quickly with a piece of clean folded rag. This is known as 'tinning the bit'.

A well-tinned bit can be spoiled by subsequent over-heating. If, by any mischance, you happen to burn the tinning, don't worry. Just clean the tip of the iron with a file to remove the scale and re-tin, as before. Don't try to carry on soldering without cleaning the iron or you will never make a successful joint.

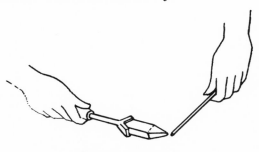

Fig 72. Soldering

There are two different ways of applying solder to a joint. In the first, and more usual way, flux is applied with a small brush to the area to be soldered, and then the heated tinned iron is used for spreading the solder along the seams, as shown in illustration 72. If the iron is sufficiently hot the bit can be charged with fresh solder from a stick held in the left hand. As soon as the solder ceases to flow freely, the iron must be re-heated or the joint will not be successful.

The second way is known as 'sweating'. If you want to use this method, coat each of the surfaces to be joined separately with a thin film of solder. Then put them together and apply sufficient heat, either with a soldering iron or a small blowtorch, to cause them to amalgamate. This kind of joint is very suitable for components that may have to take a heavy load but it will not be called for often in mobile-making.

COLOURING METAL MOBILES

Unfortunately, it is not quite so easy to put a permanent covering of paint on to the metal components of a mobile as it is on to some other materials, but these notes may be helpful.

It is a waste of time trying to apply paint to any metal surface that has the slightest trace of rust on it.

First, you will have to use one of the special de-rusting solutions that are now on the market. Most of them contain phosphoric acid, which leaves a paint-receptive film on the metal. As with any kind of pro-prietary material, follow the manufacturers' instructions implicitly.

Wipe over with a cloth soaked in white spirit (turpen-tine substitute) to remove all traces of grease, then, without any delay, apply an even coat of one of the rust-inhibiting primers sold by all ironmongers. Usually, these are based on red lead (especially suitable for iron and steel), zinc chromate (especially suitable for aluminium) or calcium plumbate (especially suitable for galvanized zinc). After that, paint with undercoat, followed by a matt, eggshell or full gloss paint in the usual way. Special anodised colours are made and sold for use on aluminium and are especially valuable when a mobile is intended to be displayed out of doors.

One word of warning: Don't rush to cover with paint any metal that has, of its own nature, an attractive surface. What could be more pleasing than—say—a piece of copper, brought to a glistening polish with steel wool, and given a coating of clear lacquer for preservation?

THE DESIGN OF METAL MOBILES

Anyone who has successfully designed mobiles in less difficult materials will find that metal offers equally exciting opportunities for creativy and inventiveness. The techniques employed may be a little more complex, but the same skill is called for in balancing shapes and arranging a satisfactory composition. Most of the difficulties of design can be overcome if the special qualities of the heavier materials are borne in mind. It is important, for instance, to choose materials of a suitable strength for every part of a metal-based mobile—an arm made of 18 S.W.G. or 20 S.W.G. galvanized iron wire may be just right for supporting two small components made (say) of tin plate a few thousandths of an inch thick, but it may well be too flimsy for use in a mobile that incorporates large copper tubes or shapes cut from sheet brass. In the upper sections of a complex metal mobile, you may find that even 12 S.W.G. wire is insufficiently strong to find a place. In these instances, steel rod and other strong and rigid materials may be called for, instead of wire. Each case has to be considered on its own merits.

9

Some further mobiles

Much of the fascination of mobile-making comes from the almost infinite variety of mobiles that can be designed and constructed from easily available materials. This chapter illustrates an assortment of mobiles, each of which has some characteristic that makes it quite unlike those already described in previous chapters. The principles on which these mobiles are based can be studied in many works by Alexander Calder and other inventive artists. No detailed instructions are given—it is taken for granted that everyone who has followed this book so far will want to devise original mobiles on his own account.

A SELF-SUPPORTING MOBILE

Fig 73. A self-supporting mobile

Illustration 73 shows how a mobile can be provided
with its own stand, so that it does not have to be suspended from any existing fitting, or positioned per-
manently in any particular place. The stand is made by
bending stout wire—14 S.W.G. or 12 S.W.G. will be
strong enough for most small mobiles. The wire can
be brought to a high polish, or, if it is preferred can be
painted any suitable colour.

ROCKING MOBILES

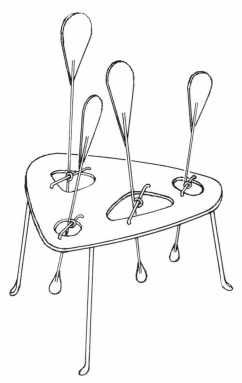

Fig 74. A rocking mobile

Illustration 74 shows a simple mobile in which a number of arms are intended to rock gently when a breeze or draught plays over them, producing the same effect as reeds or rushes will when under the influence of the wind. A small weight at the lower end of each arm provides the necessary counter-balance. A mobile of this sort may be really spectacular if it includes a sufficient number of moving components.

SWAYING MOBILES

Fig 75. A swaying mobile   *Fig 76. Another swaying mobile*

Illustration 75 shows a mobile in which some thin, springy wire is used to support components that react with great sensitivity to the gentlest breeze. Illustration 76 shows how some of the regular movement of a pendulum can be suggested by a mobile that sways provocatively on a central, whippy support. A spring steel rod, if one can be obtained, makes a splendid central swaying pillar for this kind of mobile.

SCREW MOBILES

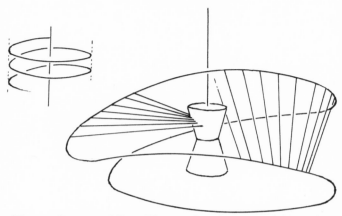

*Fig 77. Screw mobiles; The simplest form (top left) and
a more sophisticated shape under construction*

Some fascinating and delightful mobiles have been made
on the same principle as the ordinary woodscrew, the
threads of which may appear to advance when the screw
is turned, although they are not in fact moving forward.
Screw mobiles are related to, or developments of, the
simple card spiral mobile shown in illustration 17. A
particularly fine screw mobile by the British sculptor
Kenneth Martin hangs and rotates gently in the permanent collection of the Tate Gallery, London.

Two flat, painted skeletal figures shown recently in a
London exhibition caused many people who saw them
to suffer distinct feelings of dismay and nausea—the
lower part of each of their legs hung loosely from a
hinge just below the knee, and, shaking with the vibra-
tions made by each passer-by, suggested that the figure
of which it formed part was most uncannily alive. Illustration 78 shows how this particular kind of mobile,
which may have a limited appeal, may be constructed.

ARTICULATED FIGURES

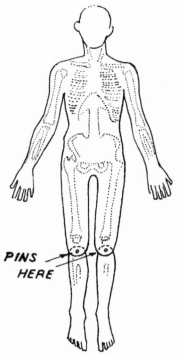

Fig 78. An articulated figure

An American artist, Pol Bury, has recently exhibited some exciting works, each of which is composed of a sizeable casing, usually wood, of a geometric and largely primitive nature, and generally of some dark, rich or sombre colour. Attached to the casing by thin transparent chords are a number of cylinders, spheres, cubes or other shapes in a variety of subtle, well-chosen colours. As a motor-driven mechanism inside the casing pulls the cords gently inwards, or, at other stages in a set cycle, releases them, the attached shapes rise, fall,

MECHANICAL MOBILES

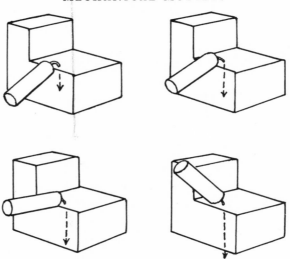

Fig 79. These drawings show how one of the cylindrical shapes described under the heading 'Mechanical Mobiles' may move. The dotted lines show the directions in which the concealed cords may pull the shape

twitch, jerk, become active, become inert, and then revive again, by turns. The movements, which cause intermittent clicks, bangs, stirrings, thuds and other noises are mostly slow and gentle, so that the occasional more violent action comes as a mildly shocking surprise. Each of Pol Bury's works of this kind seems to have a life and individual character of its own—sometimes benign, sometimes threatening, and sometimes potentially catastrophic. His experiments may suggest new wide fields of research for the truly creative mobile-maker who finds the placid action of indoor draughts and breezes insufficiently adventurous.